Bismillah hir rahman nir rahim
In the name of Allah,
The Most Gracious &
The Most Merciful

Child Loss, Bereavement and Hope: a Muslim mother's

perspective

By Farhat Amin

www.smartmuslima.com

Copyright 2021 Farhat Amin

CHILD LOSS, BEREAVEMENT & HOPE

A Muslim mother's perspective

FARHAT AMIN

"I have only created Jinn

& people that they may

worship me."

(51:56)

ACKNOWLEDGEMENTS

All praise is to Allah; I am so
grateful to Allah, who has given me
this opportunity to help my fellow Muslim
parents.
I am deeply grateful to my considerate husband, Jalaluddin
and lovely children, Musab and Rahma,
you have been my ease.

Ahmed includes the following narration from Abu Umamah who says: 'The Prophet said: how fortunate are those who say these five: Subhanallah, Alhamdulillah, La ilaha illallah, Allahu Akbar, and a pious child who passes away - if (the parent) hopes for reward.

CONTENTS

Abu Moosa al-Ash'ari, said that the Messenger of Allah (saw) said, "When the child of a person dies, Allah says to His angels: 'You have taken the soul of the child of My slave?"

They say: 'Yes.'

He says: 'You have taken the apple of his eye?'

They say: 'Yes.'

He says: 'What did My slave say?'

They say: 'He praised You and said innaa Lillaahi wa innaa ilayhi raa-ji'oon.'

And Allah says: 'Build for My slave a house in Paradise, and call it the house of praise.'

Narrated by al-Tirmidhi,

INTRODUCTION

Dear parent,

I know exactly how you are feeling. People will tell you to have sabr and trust in Allah's plan. People will expect you to behave in a certain way. I have written this book for you and me. We are parents who have lost a piece of our hearts. No one else can understand what we are going through.

Losing a baby or child, whether through miscarriage or illness, leaves so many parents lost in grief and full of unanswered questions. I personally experienced a miscarriage and also faced the loss of my teenage son. I wrote this account of my experiences to share with you how I found a way to live and learn from my great loss.

I am here to tell you that there is hope, there is a way to find peace and solace, and that way is through the healing ayat of Allah and the comforting words of our beloved Prophet Muhammad (saw). Inshallah, both the Quran and Sunnah are a balm that will soothe your heart. Together they have helped me carry on when I thought my sorrow would consume me. Inshallah, my sincere dua is that this book provides you with comfort and hope.

Let's remember each other in our duas

Your sister Farhat Amin

Abu Hassan said to Abu Hurairah,

"Two children of mine have passed away. Will you not narrate to us a Hadith from the Messenger of Allah (صلى الله عليه وسلم) that will comfort us in our loss?" He said, "Yes, their children are the children of Jannah (Paradise) and they will meet their parents and take a hold of their hands as I am taking a hold of the hem of you garment, and the child will not let go until Allah admits them all into Jannah.

(Muslim)

WHY DID I WRITE THIS BOOK?

In 1997, I began a new chapter of my life. In the short space of three months, I got married, moved to a new city, and found out I was pregnant. But then I had a miscarriage. I was a newlywed, and losing that first pregnancy was heart-breaking. I had been thrilled to be pregnant, but then things took a turn for the worse. I knew miscarriages happened, but somehow, I never thought it would happen to me. I realised that although pregnancy loss is common, studies show that about 15% of recognised pregnancies end in miscarriage, it's not often discussed openly and publicly. My faith and family got me through the trauma, and I learnt that even though I lost the pregnancy very early, it was OK to be sad, and it was OK to take as much time as I needed to heal.

Alhamdulillah, Allah subsequently blessed me with three children, two boys and a girl and, I have had 20 happy years of motherhood. In 2018 my beautiful son Muhammad Ali (Mo) passed away; he had leukaemia. He was an intelligent, witty and loving son. I miss talking to him; I miss hugging him. I miss his silly jokes. But what I know is, he was a wonderful gift from Allah, and it was time for him to go back to Allah. During both these trials, the following letter and ayahs of the Quran helped me immensely.

Prophet's (saw) letter to Mu'ad bin Jabal

Mu'adh bin Jabal was a close companion of the Prophet (saw). On the death of his son, the Prophet (saw) dictated the following letter of condolence to him.

"In the name of Allah, the Compassionate, the Merciful.

From Muhammad, the Messenger of Allah, to Mu'ad bin Jabal.

Peace be upon you!

First of all, I glorify Allah, besides Whom there is no god. Then I pray that Allah may bestow upon you a great reward for this bereavement, and grant you patience and fortitude, and give you and us the courage to be grateful to Him for His favours. The fact is that our lives and our near and dear ones are sacred gifts to us from Allah, Who has given those in our charge only temporarily. He allowed us to benefit from the gifts for as long as He willed and withdrew them as and when He willed. And in return for this (apparent loss), He will bless you with higher rewards of His special

12

favours, mercy and guidance, provided that you display fortitude for His sake and for the sake of the benefits of the Hereafter. Be patient and listen! Lest your restlessness and impatience should deprive you of reward, and you become regretful and believe with certainty that being impatient cannot bring back the dead nor can the grief be removed and that what has occurred was meant to be. " (Al-Tabarani's Mu'jam Kabir)

And We will surely test you with something of fear and hunger and a loss of wealth and lives and fruits, but give good tidings to the patient, Who, when disaster strikes them, say, "Indeed we belong to Allah, and indeed to Him, we will return. Those are the ones upon whom are blessings from their Lord and mercy. And it is those who are the [rightly] guided. (Quran 2:155-157)

Ibn Jarir, Ibn al-Mundhir and Ibn Abi Hatim, in their separate commentaries, all mention the following from Ibn Abbas; he said: "Allah informs the believers that the world is a place of tests, and He will certainly test them in it. He ordered them to exercise patience and gave them glad tiding when He said (give glad tidings to the patient). He informed (them) that if a believer subjects himself to the order of Allah, and turns to Him and recites Istirja at the time of calamity, Allah writes for him three good traits: blessings of Allah, His mercy, and achieving the right path."

The Prophet (saw) said:

Whoever recites Istirja (Surely, we belong to Allah, and to Him shall we return) at the time of a calamity, Allah helps him back from his calamity, makes his end excellent and makes for him a pious successor to please him.

I know nothing bad can ever happen to Mo; now, he is under Allah's protection. That is what gives me comfort; I have gone through many stages of grief, learnt and experienced a lot in these last four weeks. I received an email from a sister to who I had given some advice regarding the passing away of a family member, she said my words helped her, and I realised I wanted to write this book to help other parents. Furthermore, I need a place for my thoughts to rest and stop floating around in my head. I hope what I have learnt can help other grieving parents because it is heartbreaking, and you need to hear advice from a parent who has been through it.

I intend to give some of the proceeds of this book to a charity that helps sick children, my son was fortunate enough to have the best medical care, but I know that children in Muslim countries do not have that luxury. Inshallah, I will be donating proceeds to a Muslim charity that works in the Muslim world.

Surely, we belong to Allah and to Him shall we return." (Qur'an:2:156)

Child loss, bereavement and hope: a Muslim mother's perspective

Abu Hassan said to Abu Hurairah

"Two children of mine have passed away. Will you not narrate to us a Hadith

from the Messenger of Allah (صلى الله عليه وسلم) that will comfort us in our

loss?" He said, "Yes, their children are the children of Jannah (Paradise) and

they will meet their parents and take a hold of their hands as I am taking a hold

of the hem of you garment, and the child will not let go until Allah admits them

all into Jannah.

(Muslim)

WHAT I HAVE

REALISED

There is a reason why Allah decided it was time for my 15-year-old son to leave, and there is wisdom behind the decision. I will never know or understand why, as Allah is all-knowing, and I am a limited human. I can only understand what's in my reality and perception.

One of Allah's names is Al-'aleem– the All-Knowing: what is and what could be, what was and what could have been. Al-Ghazali says, "Allah's perfection lies in comprehending everything by knowledge—manifest and hidden, small and large, first and last, inception and outcome."

The difference between Allah's knowledge and human knowledge is that we must acquire knowledge based on what we see and experience. On the other hand, Allah's knowledge has no beginning or end and is not based on trial and error. Allah tells us in the Qur'an:

"And with Him are the keys of the unseen; none knows them except Him. And He knows what is on the land and in the sea. Not a leaf falls but that He knows it. And no grain is there within the darkness of the earth and no moist or dry [thing] but that it is [written] in a clear record" (Qur'an, 6:59)

In my situation, I can understand how Prophet Musa (as) felt when he met Al-Khidr. The story of this meeting between Musa (as) and Al-Khidr is related in verses 60- 82 of Surat Al-Kahf. One day, Musa (as) gave a speech to Bani Israel, and the people who heard it were profoundly moved. Someone in the crowd asked him: "O Messenger of Allah, is there another man on earth more learned than you?" Musa (as) replied: "No!"– believing, as Allah had not only given him the power of miracles and honoured him with the Torah, but He had also granted him the supreme privilege of speaking directly to Him.

Yet, in this instance, Allah chastised Musa(as) and revealed to him that no man could know all there is to know, nor would one messenger alone be the guardian of all knowledge. There would always be another with more excellent knowledge. So, Musa(as) asked Allah: "O Allah, where is this man? I would like to meet him and learn from him."

Musa (as) also asked for a sign to clarify this person's identity. Allah informed Musa (as) that he would find this wise man at the intersection of the two seas. Allah instructed him to take a live fish in a water-filled vessel, and where the fish disappeared, there he would find the man he was looking for.

Musa (as) set out on his journey, attended by a servant, who carried the vessel with the fish. When they reached the intersection of the two seas, they were tired from the long journey and stopped to rest. As they slept, the fish moved briskly in the vessel and jumped out and fell into a channel leading to the sea. It made its way out to the sea. It is said that Allah stopped the flow of water on both sides of the path created by the fish so that there became something like an archway. At the time, Musa's companion neglected to tell him that their fish had escaped. When they woke up, they continued their journey—having passed on from where Musa (as) would have encountered Al-Khidr.

Later on, in their journey, tired and hungry, Musa (as) asked his servant to bring him a meal. His servant then explained what had happened. So, they retraced their steps and were amazed to see a fantastic tunnel made of water. Musa (as) realised that this was the sign by which they were to discover Al-Khidr. Indeed, there they saw a man covered by a garment. This was Al-Khidr, the knowledgeable who Allah had meant for Musa (as) to meet. Al-Khidr is believed by scholars to have been a prophet since he followed the divine commandments of Allah.

Musa(as) approached him and greeted him. Al-Khidr asked, "Is there such a greeting in your land? Who are you?"

Musa (as) said, "I am Musa."

He said, "Are you Musa the Prophet of Allah, the Musa of the Children of Israel?"

Musa (as) said, "Yes," and added, "I have come to you so that you may teach me something of that knowledge which you have been taught." In this way, Musa(as) requested Al-Khidr to teach him the Greater Truth that Allah had granted him, as he hoped to be guided by this excellent knowledge to perform good deeds.

Al-Khidr said, "O Musa! I have some of Allah's knowledge which He has bestowed upon me but which you do not know, and you too, have some of Allah's knowledge which He has bestowed upon you, but which I do not know. Each of us has responsibilities before Allah that the other does not share. But you will not be able to have patience with me. You will not be able to accompany me when you see me execute actions that go against your better judgment. For how can you have patience about a thing you know not? I know you may justifiably denounce me, but my knowledge has been bestowed on me by Allah, and there are hidden interests in my actions, which you may not perceive."

Al-Khidr agreed to permit Musa (as) to accompany him –on certain conditions. He made Musa (as) promise he would be patient and obedient, and he must not question him about the reason behind any of the actions he was about to see.

Al-Khidr emphasised that Musa (as) should not ask him about what he might find distasteful until he initiated the discussion and gave an explanation. Based on this understanding, the two began their journey.

Musa (as) and Al-Khidr set out walking on the seashore. A boat sailed by, and they asked the sailors to take them on board. The crew recognised Al-Khidr and welcomed them both warmly. They would be pleased to have Al-Khidr as their passenger, and they agreed to take them both to their destination without any fare. When they were on board the boat, a sparrow came and stood on the edge of the boat and dipped its beak once or twice into the sea. Al-Khidr said to Musa (as): "O Musa! My knowledge and your knowledge have not decreased Allah's knowledge except as much as this sparrow has decreased the water of the sea with its beak." Unexpectedly, Al-Khidr pulled up a plank that disabled the boat. Then, he roughly patched it up again.

Musa (as) was shocked and could not stop himself from asking: "What have you done? These people took us on board, charging us nothing, yet you have deliberately damaged their boat to drown its passengers. Verily, you have done a terrible thing." Al-Khidr replied: "Did I not tell you that you would not be able to remain patient with me?" Musa (as) immediately regretted what he had said and replied: "Call me not to account for what I have forgotten, and do not be hard upon me for my fault." Musa (as) realised the mistake he had made, so he implored Al-Khidr not to let his outburst make Al-Khidr exclude him from being allowed to accompany him further.

The two left the boat, and while they were walking, they saw a young boy playing with other boys. He was the finest and most handsome of all the boys. Al-Khidr singled him out, and without provocation, he took the boy away and killed him. When he observed this, Musa (as) was horrified. He perceived the killing as unjustified, so he confronted Al-Khidr, "Have you slain an innocent person who had harmed no one? Truly a foul (unheard of) thing have you done!"

Al-Khidr reprimanded him and reiterated that he had correctly assumed earlier that Musa (as) would have no patience with him. Upon hearing this, Prophet Musa was ashamed and realised that he had violated his trust with Al-Khidr. Musa realised that he must refrain from arguing and further questioning, or he would undoubtedly be deprived of any further knowledge and benefit from this wise one. He fervently pleaded, "If I ask you anything after this, keep me not in your company, and you will have received an excuse for sending me away."

Next, they came upon a village. Here the two travellers requested food and shelter. As per the custom of the day, wayfarers should be welcomed into the fold of any home or town they passed through, and the inhabitants were to be honoured with the provision of food and a resting place. However, the people of this village rejected the universal rule of hospitality towards the strangers. Their manners were devoid of any basic courtesy and proved extremely rude in their outright refusal to offer food in any form to their guests.

Upon leaving the village, the two came upon a wall that was on the point of collapse. To Musa's utter surprise, Al-Khidr began to repair the crumbling wall and fortified it by setting it upright again. Musa (as) was unable to contain his anger. He was outraged that Al-Khidr had rewarded these arrogant people by helping them. The least he could have done was to ask for payment for the job so that they could have bought some food with the money.

At this point, Al-Khidr said: "You agreed after the boy was killed that if you asked me any explanation after that, you would not accompany me any further. So, this is the parting of the ways between you and me."

Al-Khidr was now ready to explain the cause of all these seemingly irrational acts, and what had prompted him to do them:

As for the boat, he explained, it belonged to poor people working on the sea, there was an oppressive king who was seizing every ship by force, Al-Khidr wished to save the boat by inflicting a defect on it, as that action would ultimately save their source of income.

As for the boy killed without provocation, his rebellious nature and arrogance, as known to Al-Khidr, would have led his righteous parents not only away from the true faith but towards disbelief and sin due to their love for him. Al-Khidr knew that Allah would bless them with another child who would be purer, more virtuous and merciful.

As for the wall, there are two orphan boys in the town, and a treasure belonging to them was under it. Their father had been a pious man, and they were entitled to these riches. Allah intended that they attain their age of full strength and take out their treasure as a mercy from Him. These were Al-Khidr's interpretation of those (things) over which Musa (as) could not be patient.

Al-Khidr said that he had done none of these actions on his initiative or his authority. He declared that they were done under divine guidance in all three cases, though they appeared to Musa (as) inexplicable and perhaps even cruel. Allah had prevailed upon him to perform the acts for a definite reason. He concluded by saying, "Such is the interpretation of those things over which you were unable to hold patience."

The lesson I gained from this narration was that asking why my son passed away was futile. I needed to have trust in Allah's plan and be patient. Allah knows of our pain and will reward us for our patience. Alhamdulillah, He promises us Jannah if we have sabr. And (He) will reward them for what they patiently endured (with) a garden (in Paradise) and silk (garments). (Quran 76:12)

When a person's child dies, Allah, the Most High, asks His angels, 'Have you taken the life of the child of My slave?' They reply in the affirmative. Allah then asks them, 'Have you taken the fruit of his heart?' They respond in the affirmative. Thereupon He asks, 'What has My slave said? 'The Angels say, 'He praised you and said 'Inna lillahi wa inna ilayhi raji'oon (To Allah we belong and to Him we will return)' At that Allah replies, 'Build a home for my slave in Jannah and call it 'Bayt-ul-Hamd' (Home of Praise)'. (Tirmidhi)

I was so happy when I read the following hadith,

"By Him in whose hands is my life, a child will pull its mother to Jannah if she is patient". (Ibn Majah)

Inshallah, our children are a source of Paradise and please take comfort from the following hadith Samura bin Jundub narrates:

Allah's Apostle often asked his companions, 'Did any of you see a dream?' So, dreams would be narrated to him by those whom Allah wished to tell. One morning, the Prophet Muhammed (saw) said, 'Last night, two persons came to me (in a dream) and woke me up and said to me 'Proceed!' I set out with them....'

He (saw) mentioned things and places that he had seen, and then he said, 'We proceeded, and we reached a garden of deep green dense vegetation, having all sorts of spring colours. Amid the garden, there was a very tall man, and I could hardly see his head because of his great height, and around him, there were children in such a large number as I have never seen. I said to my companions, 'Who is this?' They replied, 'Proceed! Proceed!'

Then among the things that the two companions (angels) said to him (saw) was: 'The tall man whom you saw in the garden is Ibrahim (as) and the children around him are those children who die with Al-Fitrah (the Islamic Faith).' (Bukhari)

"It was narrated from Mu'aadh ibn Jabal that the Prophet (saw) said:

"By the One in Whose hand is my soul, the miscarried foetus will drag his mother by his umbilical cord to Paradise, if she (was patient and) sought reward (for her loss)."

Narrated by Ibn Maajah

WAS I A GOOD PARENT?

The day after Muhammad passed away, I started searching my memories; I needed to know if I had been a good mum to Mo. I kept asking my family, and they reassured me that I was a good mother. I looked at photos and saw that, yes, Mo used to be sitting next to me smiling. My eldest son told me, "Mama, Muhammad loved you so much." I know I was a good mum, and I wouldn't change how I raised him: I have no regrets.

You can't change the past, don't torment yourself about your past actions. No parent is perfect, don't beat yourself up about the times you told off your child. What you can do, is change the way you treat your other children or nieces and nephews. Read about how the Prophet Muhammad (saw) was with his children and follow his example. The only thing we can do is to learn from our mistakes.

Could I have done more to help my son? Should I have taken him to the doctor's earlier? If only I had got him a blood test earlier, then they could have started treatment sooner? I'm sure you have asked yourself similar questions.

I quickly realised that asking these questions achieves nothing except for making me feel guilty and upset. Mothers are very good at feeling guilty; we never think we are doing enough for our children. Society loves to blame us for everything; we can never win whether we stay at home or go to work. I stopped asking these questions when I remembered that Allah had already decided the day Mo would pass away. As the following hadith mentions,

"On the authority of Abu Abdul Rahmaan Abdullah ibn Masood (may Allah be pleased with him) who said: The Messenger of Allah (saw) and he is the truthful, the believed, narrated to us: Verily, each of you is brought together in his mother's abdomen for forty days in the form of a drop of fluid. Then it is a clinging object for a similar [period]. After that, it is a lump looking like it has been chewed for a similar [period]. The angel is then sent to him, and he breathes into him the spirit. He is also commanded to issue four decrees: to record his sustenance, his life span, his deeds and [whether he will be] unhappy [by entering Hell] or happy [by entering Paradise]. I swear by Allah, other than whom there is no God, certainly one of you will perform the deeds of the people of

Paradise until there is between him and Paradise except an arm's length, and then what has been recorded will overtake him. He shall perform the deeds of the people of Hell and enter it. And, certainly, one of you will definitely perform the acts of the people of Hell until there is not between him and Hell except an arm's length, and then what has been recorded for him will overtake him. He shall perform the deeds of the people of Paradise and enter it." (Bukhari and Muslim)

I know I could not have changed the day my son passed away. One of the many reasons why I believe Allah is my creator is because I know he has control over the day I was born, and the day I will die. As a mother, the only thing I could do was make my son comfortable and take care of him when he was ill. I am blessed that I got to do that for a week when he was at home, and I am grateful that I got to spend the night with him before he passed away.

And remember when your Lord proclaimed, 'If you are grateful, I will certainly give you more. But if you are ungrateful, surely My punishment is severe." (Quran14:7)

I must remember that nothing can harm my son now. My child is in Allah's protection. Allah loves him more than I ever could, and that is a fact. What is the worst fear that we have for our children?

That something awful might happen to them? That they could get hurt? Now that my son is with Allah, nothing can harm him. Nothing bad will ever happen to him again. Whenever I feel upset about his passing away, I visualise him snugly tucked up in a soft, warm bed in heaven, sleeping peacefully. I don't think about when he was in the hospital; I don't have any photos of him when he was ill.

When I want to remember him, I look at photos and videos of him smiling and playing; that's how we should remember our children. Don't dwell on the illness that your child may have gone through. I refuse to talk about the details of my son's illness as it's like I'm reliving that time, and I don't think that's a healthy thing to do. You shouldn't feel like you have to give the details of your child's last few days to anyone. People should understand that it's upsetting and should respectfully let you grieve in your own way.

Child Loss, Bereavement and Hope: a Muslim mother's perspective

Child loss, bereavement and hope: a Muslim mother's perspective

Said ibn Mansur records in his Sunan from Anas, "A person who lost his son was consoled by the Prophet (saw) with the words:

"Will it not please you that he will be at your side on the day of Qiyamah, when it will be said to him, 'Enter Jannah', and he will say, 'Oh my lord and my parents?' and he will continue to intercede on behalf of his parents until Allah accept his intercession on behalf of his parents, and enters them all into Jannah."

HOW I CHOSE TO GRIEVE

After the second day that my son passed away, I decided that I wouldn't meet many people, and I was not going to explain how my son had passed away as it was too upsetting and painful. I don't know of any ayah or hadith that says a mother must publicly show her grief or share her pain. In Asian culture, there is a stereotype of a grieving mother. I decided I was not going to be that grieving mother. I quickly realised that I needed to have only my close family and friends near me. They were the ones who could support me. I only wanted to speak to Islamically minded people, i.e. people who would give me good Islamic advice. So, please remember it's OK to say you don't want to meet people, you don't have to talk to strangers about your loss politely, don't feel compelled into doing what is culturally expected of you. Only care what Allah thinks, and inshallah, you will be OK.

Our beloved Prophet (saw) experienced many losses in his lifetime, including six children and his grandchildren, too. When Zainab's (ra) son was dying, she called for her father (saw).

The child was lifted to the Messenger of Allah (saw) while his breath was disturbed in his chest. On seeing that, the eyes of the Prophet (saw) streamed with tears. Sa'd bin 'Ubadah said "O Messenger of Allah! What is this?" He (saw) replied, "It is compassion which Allah has placed in the hearts of His slaves; Allah is compassionate only to those among His slaves who are compassionate (to others)." (Bukhari)

The Prophet Muhammad (saw) also cried when his son Ibrahim died as an infant. Ibrahim was in his last breaths, and the eyes of Allah's Messenger started shedding tears. Abdur Rahman bin 'Auf said, "O Allah's Messenger (saw), even you are weeping!" He (saw) said, "O Ibn 'Auf, this is mercy". Then he (saw) wept more and said, "The eyes are shedding tears, and the heart is grieved, and we will not say except what pleases our Lord. O, Ibrahim! Indeed, we are grieved by your separation".

Inshallah, remember Allah in your sorrow as illustrated in the following hadith, Ibn' Umar (ra) narrated:The Messenger of Allah (saw) visited Sa'd bin 'Ubadah during his illness. He was accompanied by 'Abdur-Rahman bin 'Auf, Sa'd bin Abu Waqqas and 'Abdullah bin Mas'ud. The Messenger of Allah (saw) began to weep. When his companions saw this, their tears also started flowing. He (saw), said, "Do you not hear, Allah does not punish for the shedding of tears or the grief of the heart but punishes or bestows mercy for the utterances of this (and he pointed to his tongue) (Al-Bukhari)

Allah knows of our pain and will reward us greatly for having patience. In fact, He promises Jannah for those who adopt sabr.

And (He) will reward them for what they patiently endured (with) a garden (in Paradise) and silk (garments).(Quran 76:12)

When baby Ibrahim [the Prophet's son] fell seriously ill, his state worsened, and it became apparent that he would not live long. The news deeply shocked the Prophet, so much so that he felt that his legs could no longer carry him. He proceeded immediately and arrived in time to bid farewell to his son, who was dying on his mother's lap. The Prophet trembled as he held baby Ibrahim close. His heart was torn apart by this tragedy, and his face mirrored his inner pain. Choking with sorrow, he said: "O Ibrahim, against the judgement of Allah we cannot benefit you at all," and then fell silent.

Baby Ibrahim passed away gradually while his weeping mother and aunt looked on helplessly. With tears flowing from his blessed eyes, the Prophet said: "Verily, to Allah we belong and to Him we shall return. Tears flow from the eyes, and hearts are full of sorrow, but we only say that which pleases our Lord. O Ibrahim, we are indeed grieved by your passing away."

REMEMBERING MUHAMMAD

Muhammad was in Year 11, and he used to talk about school and his friends, but I had never met them. His friends, teachers and whole year group were deeply affected by the news of his sudden passing away. Alhamdulillah, his school was very supportive and gave students time off on the day of his funeral. Muhammad's Form Tutor and Head of Year came to the janaza at the masjid with many of his friends. Alhamdulillah, we got to speak to them, and they were the sincerest, nicest bunch of Muslim teenage boys I had ever met. We really wanted to know about their memories of Muhammad, so we asked them to come and visit us at home.

Alhamdulillah, his friends came to our home on the third day. I was surprised by the sheer number; I think there were about thirty, they all respectfully sat on the floor in our dining room. I had not wanted to see anyone that day, but once Muhammad's friends began sharing their stories with us, my mood lifted. They really did love him like a brother; they said he was known as the boy who prayed salah, he would encourage others to come to jummah at school, he had no enemies, he was a witty, sharp and loyal friend. I was so proud to hear my son had been a positive influence in the lives of so many of his friends. I cannot explain how much talking and laughing with his friends that afternoon helped me.

Two weeks later, Muhammad's school invited us to a memorial assembly. Alhamdulillah, Muhammad's uncles, aunties, and cousins all came to the assembly as well. Entering the school was very hard for my husband and me as the last time we had visited was for Muhammad's parent evening. The assembly had a charming Islamic atmosphere; his close friends had nasheeds playing while photos of Muhammad were displayed. The most moving aspect for all my family was listening to the heartfelt tributes that his friends delivered. I know it was hard for them to stand up in front of so many students, but they did that for their brother. I thank Allah that Muhammad has so many kind-hearted, sincere friends, and I got to meet them; they will remain in my duas forever. I want to share the eulogies that Muhammad's friends gave at his memorial assembly.

"Muhammed Patel was the epitome of a good friend. He was unique and a pure-hearted person; you gave us a new perspective on life and made us understand that it is too precious to waste. He was always positive, and we could always rely on him to make us laugh and smile. His jokes never got old, and his sarcasm was the best. He was intelligent and would always beat us in tests and debates, but he would always remain humble. He would always be there to lift you up when you were feeling down. He was gifted in sports and would beat us every time so effortlessly. When the news of you leaving us came through, the entire year was distraught. It goes to show that he was truly a special person and was always good to those around and kept the best intentions at heart. The memories we shared are unforgettable. We will cherish them forever and will never forget you, and you will remain in our hearts for as long as we live. We hope to meet you again in heaven, and we hope you are resting well, and we pray you remember us because it's impossible for us to forget you."

Ijaz

"For all you were to us in life and all the joy you brought,
your memory is with us in every single thought.The pain we felt at losing you will never go away, but knowing that you're in a heart helps us through each day. When you were here, we always felt that nothing could go wrong, but you're still our inspiration, and your memory keeps us strong.

And though our heart is heavy, it's always full of love,

and that's enough to comfort us while you're in heaven above.

We cried when you passed away, some of us crying still today,

although we loved you dearly, but it wasn't enough to make you stay.

Muhammed Patel was a young man who shared many jokes; he was indeed a humble soul. His family made him so happy and proud everyone he met; he would tell them aloud. Muhammed Patel has left so many happy thoughts in our hearts; we still find it hard to believe that he is gone. We are heartbroken that Muhammad is no longer here. When we think of him, we always shed a tear. People tell us that the pain will stop in time, but we will always miss the times we had with our dear Muhammed Patel. Now it's time for us to say goodbye; he will be looking down on us, wishing us not to cry, but this is what I will say to Muhammad as a guarantee, in our hearts a memory, and there will always be."

Khushal

"Muhammad Ali Patel, our greatest friend left this world, returned to his maker, our greatest friend went now waiting for his parents at the gates (of Jannah)

You looked so peaceful as if you could change a life with your beautiful face.

And you did

Changed our lives, made us better, in a way perfected us, made us more efficient we owe all these things to you; you brought us closer to our maker, Allah.

Allah help him

Allah save him

Allah bless him

The least we can do is celebrate your life, celebrate all the memories we had

Even if it's discussing Bill Khan or even talking about Paan

Your life is cherished; we'll never forget you; you're a loving son, brother, and brother even after the end

A brother to his amazing siblings who have supported us and helped us through the pain

A brother to all of our friends, especially the ones who you made awake. Allah took you when your time came; only Allah knows when we will join you in the grave.

Muhammad Ali Patel

Such a beautiful name."

-Qasim Khan

"The smile, how can I forget the smile, running a mile into our hearts.

Neutral he was as he helped anyone that came along, how can I forget when he lay at ease going to the All-Mighty in peace. Hoping we meet you, we pray, we pray.

We can't help but feel you were taken too soon.

All we can do is look at the moon, hoping we'll reunite in heaven.

Days are long, sadness around.

All our friends surround

Sharing your jokes with your family

Had the whole room laughing, sharing your personality

His death humbled us all.

And his memories tumbled out of our hearts.

Patel did nothing wrong.

Lucky to have parents so strong

No way we could forget him

All we think is how to help him.

Knowing that Allah takes the best of us

Our friend our brother left us

The afterlife is next.

Where he'll shine bright

Patel, you'll always be in our prayers

You'll always be in our mind."

Abu-Bakr Hussain

Muhammad Patel

"I will never forget the jokes that we used to share,

I miss you so much, and you shall always remain in my prayer.

Having a best friend like you is extremely rare,

I'm glad I had you because my memories with you will never disappear.

You were someone who I could easily talk to,

You always had a solution to a problem that any of us went through,

Everything about you was always so true

You were incredibly gifted and one of a kind,
You're amazing smile always made us feel fine,
The clever thoughts that always crossed your mind,
Always used to stop us from falling behind.

The way you played football was something that I admired,
You always dribbled past defenders and often made them tired.
Your football skills are something that we all desire,
Because every time we played, you were always on fire.

I will miss you, and you will forever remain in my heart,
Although, right now we are apart
Soon, we shall reunite in heaven and be together.
And that will make me more happy than ever."
Adil Asghar

Child Loss, Bereavement and Hope: a Muslim mother's perspective

It was narrated in al-Saheehayn that there is a special reward for the person whose child dies, but he bears that with patience and hopes for reward. It was narrated from Abu Sa'eed (may Allah be pleased with him) that the women said to the Prophet (peace and blessings of Allah be upon him): "Give us a day (to teach us)," So he preached to them and said, "Any woman who loses three of her children, they will be a shield for her against the Fire." A woman said, "And two?" He said, "And two."

(Bukhari)

WAKE UP CALL

I never expected my son to pass away so quickly. No parent ever expects that their child will pass away before them. The shock and trauma I went through was mentally and physically exhausting. It was very sudden. We took Muhammad to Luton hospital late in the evening, thinking he had an infection. But when the blood test results came back, the doctor, a young Indian woman, told us he had blood cancer. Her words pierced my heart.

I instantly burst into tears as a few months earlier, my father had died of cancer, and I instantly thought of him. I kept thinking, how am I going to tell Muhammad he has cancer? He will be so upset. How can I protect him from this pain?

After wiping our tears and putting on a brave face, my husband and I told him. We emphasised that he would get treatment at a specialist hospital, and we would be with him all the time. In the middle of the night, Muhammad was rushed to Addenbrooke's hospital in Cambridge; they wanted to immediately begin his treatment. Alhamdulilah, I went with him in the ambulance, holding his hand, trying to comfort him.

Reliving and describing the last two days in the hospital with Muhammad is too painful. I can share with you the last words my son said to me whilst still coherent and not on painkillers. I had been up with him most of the night, and he softly said to me, " Jazakhallah Khair Mama" Alhamdulillah, Allah truly blessed me with a grateful son. The next day he passed away; my husband, my eldest son, my daughter, and I were all in the room when the angel of death came and returned Muhammad's soul to his creator.

If I wasn't Muslim and didn't have the Quran and Sunnah to help me make sense of Muhammad's death, then I think I would have had a complete breakdown. I can see why non-Muslim grieving parents turn to drink or drugs to drown their sorrows. I feel immense sympathy for them. But in contrast, I understood what had just happened; my husband and I did not blame the doctors or get angry with them because they could not "save" our son. We knew this was meant to happen. Our faith gave us perspective.

Coming back home from the hospital without Mo was very difficult. It's like he had disappeared; all his clothes and books and things were still in his room: but he was not. Our home felt empty, and quiet.

Mo's passing away was a wake-up call. Suddenly, my mortality had become a stark reality. If my 15-year-old son could pass away in the blink of an eye, in front of me, then so can I, and I will. This experience has made me evaluate how I spend my time, what I watch, who I talk to, how much Quran I read and what I say. I know inshallah my son is on his way to Paradise, that is a blessing, so my dream is to meet him there. My life has become more focused. I used to spend a lot of time worrying about my business and thinking about how I can earn more money. But now I want to spend my time worshipping and obeying my creator, who I am definitely going to meet. Now is the time to take stock of my life and ponder on how I am preparing for the next life, which is eternal. As Allah says, "It is he who created death and life to test which of you are best indeed, for he is the Almighty, the Forgiving." (Quran 67:2)

Child loss, bereavement and hope: a Muslim mother's perspective

Abu Huraira reported: The Messenger of Allah, peace and blessings be upon him, said, "If Allah wills good for someone, He afflicts him with trials."

Bukhari

HOW TO BEHAVE WHEN VISITING GRIEVING PARENTS

U nless you have gone through this yourself, you will likely have very little knowledge on how to comfort or even talk to a friend or relative who has. When people hear about the death of a child, they feel shocked and upset and want to immediately visit and comfort the parents. What you need to think is what is the best way to help the parents? The purpose of your visit should be selfless and only for the family's good.

Before you visit text, another family member and ask them if it is a good time to visit. I would recommend doing lots of dua for the family and sending them a text which will include hadith and ayah of Quran that will give them solace and hope. If you live nearby, then send food to the family. Take disposable cups and plates to them, so they do not have to worry about cleaning up.

When you are visiting the family, do not ask them lots of questions, I did not want to answer questions about my son. Avoid curiosity about the circumstances around the child's death; it will upset the parents. Ali ibn Husayn reported: The Messenger of Allah, peace and blessings be upon him, said, "Verily, among excellence in Islam is for a man to leave what does not concern him."

Even in my state of extreme grief, I could tell those whose curiosity overcame their desire to be sensitive to my feelings. An unintentional tactless comment or act in no way undermines the incredible love and support a family member or friend provides. However, it's tough to know what to say or do to provide comfort and support for bereaved parents even with the best intentions. Ask yourself whether what you want to say will make the parent feel better; if you're in any doubt, it is safer to say nothing at all.

Take a copy of the Quran with you and read it whilst you are there. Give your condolences in a way that helps the family, not in a way that will upset them. It is very draining for a parent to be constantly crying and be in a room full of people who are crying; it is better to be in a room full of people reading the Quran and doing dua. Don't stay for too long, as the family members will be emotionally and physically exhausted.

Alhamdulillah, I received many texts and emails with lovely duas from sisters I had known years ago, and so did my husband. I know all the duas helped me get through the first few weeks.

I would recommend buying a set of Yasin books which include the English translation. I wish I had had them when I had visitors coming to my home. I now have them to prepare the next time a family member passes away to give them to visitors to read.

According to a report narrated by al- Anas ibn Maalik (may Allah be pleased with him) said: The Messenger of Allah (saw) said: "There is no Muslim who loses three of his children before they reach the age of puberty, but Allah will admit him to Paradise by virtue of His Mercy towards them."

(Bukhari)

PRACTICAL ADVICE FOR GRIEVING PARENTS

It's normal to feel deep sadness and grief after a miscarriage or the loss of a child. For some parents, these feelings can lead to depression. Depression, also known as major depressive disorder, is a mental illness that causes persistent and intense feelings of sorrow for extended periods. Many people with depression also lose interest in activities they once enjoyed and have difficulty performing daily tasks. If you are experiencing such feelings, please speak to your GP and seek help.

I want to share some practical strategies that I have begun to incorporate into my daily routine. Alhamdulillah, they have helped me manage my feelings and be more appreciative and grateful for the blessings I have in my life. They are based on positive psychology. "Positive psychology is the scientific study of what makes life most worth living." (Peterson, 2008)

People tend to think that it's only about looking at the upside of life while trying to avoid negative things, but it goes way beyond this superficial notion. When you implement positive practices from this field, you don't disregard the bad stuff – you learn how to deal with it more resiliently while keeping the focus on the positive. You gently tip the balance toward a greater sense of well-being.

You can't outrun the bad things in life, but you can counterbalance them by adding good stuff into the mix. Because of the negativity bias, we tend to give more weight to bad things and see positive things as neutral or ordinary – not special. However, when we learn to refocus our attention by becoming aware of all the good in our lives, inshallah, we can rewire our brains over time.

Pray your salah, read Quran and make dua

I cannot describe the level of comfort salah gave me. When you, make sujood you can directly pour your heart out to Allah and ask Him to help you. Recite Quran regularly, especially the ayah describing Jannah, as that is where our children will be living. Raise your hands to The Most Merciful and ask Him to guide you. Prophet Muhammad (saw) said,

"There is nothing more honourable with Allah than supplication." (Tirmidhi)

Raise your hands in dua, knowing that nothing can make you happier than seeking the pleasure of Allah. When you put Allah at the centre of your life, that's when you will be truly happy.

Gain Knowledge

The Messenger of Allah (saw), said: "Seeking knowledge is an obligation upon every Muslim." (Ibn Mājah)

An excellent place to begin is learning and knowing the attributes of Allah. This will allow you to understand more about Him, so you will learn to put your trust in and depend on Him. Hence, you will not be overwhelmed with sadness when you think about your child and remain calm and patient.

Meditate

Take just five minutes each day to watch your breath go in and out. While you do so, try to remain patient. If you find your mind drifting, just slowly bring it back to focus. Meditation takes practice, but it's one of the most powerful happiness interventions. Studies show that in the minutes right after meditating, we experience feelings of calm and contentment and heightened awareness and empathy. And, research even shows that regular meditation can permanently rewire the brain to raise happiness levels, lower stress, even improve immune function.

Commit conscious acts of kindness

Acts of altruism—giving to friends and strangers alike—decrease stress and strongly contributes to enhanced mental health. To try this yourself, pick one day a week and make a point of committing two acts of kindness. But if you want to reap the psychological benefit, make sure you do these things deliberately and consciously—you can't just look back over the last 24 hours and declare your acts post hoc. ("Oh yeah, I held the door for that man coming out of the shop. That was kind.") And they need not be grand gestures, either. One of my favourite acts is regularly giving clothes to the charity shop. I donated a lot of my son's clothes to Muslim charities.

Find something to look forward to

Often, the most enjoyable part of an activity is the anticipation. You probably do not want to socialise with your friends, so instead, put something on the calendar— even if it's a month or a year down the road, i.e. go on Umrah. Then whenever you need a boost of happiness, remind yourself about it. Anticipating future rewards can light up the pleasure centres in your brain much as the actual reward will.

Infuse positivity into your surroundings

Our physical environment can have an enormous impact on our mindset and sense of well-being. While we may not always have complete control over our surroundings, we can make specific efforts to infuse them with positivity. Think about your home: What feelings does it inspire? People who have natural images or pictures of loved ones aren't just decorating—they're ensuring a hit of positive emotion each time they glance in that direction.

Remove negative influences

We can change our surroundings to keep negative emotions at bay. Any people who make you feel negative, stop meeting them or decrease the time you have to interact with them. For that matter, you might also reduce your social media consumption; studies have shown that the less harmful media we watch, specifically violent, grim media, the happier we are. This doesn't mean shutting ourselves off from the real world or ignoring problems. Psychologists have found that people who watch less TV are more accurate judges of life's risks and rewards than those who subject themselves to the tales of crime, tragedy, and death that appear night after night on the news and TV shows.

Spend money on others

Contrary to the famous saying, money can buy happiness, but only if used to do things instead of simply having things. While the positive feelings we get from material objects are frustratingly fleeting, spending money on experiences, especially ones with other people, produces positive emotions that are both more meaningful and more lasting. Spending money on other people also boosts happiness, for instance, by treating a friend to lunch, volunteering, or giving sadaqah.

Go walking regularly

Making time to go outside on a nice day also delivers a huge advantage; one study found that spending 20 minutes outdoors in good weather not only boosted positive mood but broadened thinking and improved working memory. Eating a balanced diet, getting enough sleep can also help increase your energy level and ward off negative thoughts.

Start journaling

I found the simple act of writing my thoughts down daily highly therapeutic. Journaling can be effective for many different reasons. It can help you clear your head, help you make sense of your feelings and even reduce the effects of stress! This book is essentially a collection of the pages I wrote in my journal. Here's how you can begin journaling:

- Write at least once a day.
- Give yourself some time to reflect after writing.
- If you're writing to overcome trauma, don't feel obligated to write about a specific traumatic event—journal about what feels right at the moment.
- Structure the writing, however, feels right to you.
- Keep your journal private; it's for your eyes only—not your spouse, not your family, not your friends.

Count your existing blessings

Allah the Exalted said: So remember Me, I will remember you. Be thankful to Me, and do not be ungrateful. (2:152)

Your Lord has proclaimed: If you are grateful, I will increase you, but if you are ungrateful, then My punishment is severe. (14:7)

3 Good Things

The positive psychology exercise 3 Good Things develops gratefulness. It asks you to focus on three good things that happened to you on a given day. In the beginning, you might find it challenging to come up with something that you consider "good enough" to be on your list – that's perfectly normal and no reason for self-criticism. You will find that it gets easier over time and that once you think of one good thing, more good things tend to follow. It's best to do the exercise daily for 10 minutes until it becomes a habit.

For each good thing, give it a title (a sentence that summarises what happened), then write down as much detail as possible. Try to recall how you felt during the event and consider how it makes you feel now. The final step is to write about how this event came about – what caused it?

For example, a 3 Good Things entry might look like this:

All my family came to visit me and cooked us dinner.

My brothers, sister, sisters-in-laws, nieces, and nephews all came round; we read Surah Yasin together and did dua for Muhammad; the delicious smell of their lovely food filled the room with warmth.The event made me feel grateful for my family, and when I think back, I still feel warm and happy inside.It happened because all my family members are generous, thoughtful, loving people, and it reminded me of the ayah "Verily, with every hardship comes ease." (Quran 94:6)

Improving your character and relationships with your spouse and family

Aisha reported: The Messenger of Allah, (saw), said: Verily, the most complete of believers in faith are those with the best character and who are most kind to their families. (Tirmidhi).

Now is the perfect time to focus on developing a stronger relationship with your spouse and family. Without my family I would not have been able to cope with the loss of my son.

Make dua for other parents

The Prophet ﷺ said: "No Muslim servant supplicates for his brother behind his back but that the angel says: And for you the same." (Muslim). A powerful remedy to brokenness, sadness, and melancholy is to give and practice generosity of the self. And from all the gifts we have been blessed with, one of the greatest and most mutually beneficial is the gift of du'a. When you are feeling down, start actively making sincere du'a for others. Make a list of people, be generous with your time and words, and don't even once worry about yourself. Let the angels do that for you. One of the best ways to take your mind off your problems is to do dua for a fellow Muslim.

Child Loss, Bereavement and Hope: a Muslim mother's perspective

"Know you not that Allah knows all

that is in heaven and on the earth?"

(22:70)

UNDERSTANDING PREDESTINATION & FREE WILL

Qadr means that Allah has decreed everything that happens in the universe according to His prior knowledge and the dictates of His will. He is the Creator of the universe, and knows how and when everyone will pass away.

Qadr is an article of faith

It was reported on the authority of Umar, who said:

"While we were one day sitting with the Messenger of Allah (saw), there appeared before us a man dressed in extremely white clothes and with very black hair. No traces of journeying were visible on him, and none of us knew him. He sat down close by the Prophet, rested his knee against his thighs, and said, "O Muhammad! Inform me about Islam."

The Messenger of Allah (saw) said, "Islam is that you should testify that there is no deity except Allah and that Muhammad is His Messenger, that you should perform salah, pay the Zakah, fast during Ramadan, and perform Hajj to the House if you are able to do so."

The man said, "You have spoken truly." We were astonished at his questioning him (the Messenger) and telling him that he was right, but he went on to say, "Inform me about Iman."

He answered, "It is that you believe in Allah and His angels and His Books and His Messengers and in the Last Day, and in Qadr (fate), both in its good and in its evil aspects." He said, "You have spoken truly."

Then he (the man) said, "Inform me about Ihsaan." He (the Messenger of Allah) answered, "It is that you should serve Allah as though you could see Him, for though you cannot see Him yet (know that), He sees you."

He said, "Inform me about the Hour." He (the Messenger of Allah) said, "About that, the one questioned knows no more than the questioner." So he said, "Well, inform me about the signs thereof." He said, "They are that the slave-girl will give birth to her mistress, that you will see the barefooted, naked, destitute, the herdsmen of the sheep (competing with each other) in raising lofty buildings."

Thereupon the man went off. I waited a while, and then he (the Messenger of Allah) said, "O Umar, do you know who that ques-

70

tioner was?" I replied, "Allah and His Messenger know better." He said, "That was Jibril (the Angel Gabriel). He came to teach you your religion." (Muslim)

Belief in Qadr includes:

- The belief that Allah knows all things, in general, and in detail, whether in regards to His actions or the actions of His slaves.

- The belief that Allah has written that in al-Lawh al-Mahfooz (the Book of Decrees). Al-Lawh al-Mahfooz is a divine creation of Allah.

Concerning these two matters, Allah says:

"Know you not that Allah knows all that is in heaven and on the earth? Verily, it is (all) in the Book (Al-Lawh Al-Mahfooz). Verily, that is easy for Allah" (22:70)

In Saheeh Muslim, it is narrated that 'Abd-Allah ibn 'Amr ibn al-'Aas said: I heard the Messenger of Allaah (saw) say: "Allah wrote down the decrees of creation fifty thousand years before He created the heavens and the earth."

And the Prophet (saw) said: "The first thing that Allah created was the Pen (al-Qalam), and He said to it, 'Write!' It said, 'O Lord, what should I write?' He said: 'Write down the decrees of all things until the Hour begins." Narrated by Abu Dawood

- The belief that whatever happens only happens by Allah's will – whether that has to do with His actions or the actions of created beings. Allah says concerning His actions:

"And your Lord creates whatsoever He wills and chooses" (28:68)

"He it is Who shapes you in the wombs as He wills" (3:6)

Islam is submission to God's will

God willed the universe and everything in it into being. When He means to create anything, He simply commands: "Be", and it is. Nothing happens except by the will of God. A Muslim is a person who intentionally accepts whatever is willed by Allah, whether it is pleasant or unpleasant.

Free will

Belief in Qadr does not contradict the idea that a person has free will concerning actions in which they have free choice. Allah has given human beings the ability to choose to accept Allah's guidance or reject it. We will either enter Jannah or Jahannam based on the choices we make in this life.

"And we showed him (the man) the two paths (of good and bad)." (90:10)

Allah says concerning man's will:

"That is (without a doubt) the True Day. So, whosoever wills, let him seek a place with (or a way to) His Lord (by obeying Him in this worldly life)!" (78:39)

And He says concerning man's ability:

"So keep your duty to Allah and fear Him as much as you can" (64:16)

"Allah burdens not a person beyond his scope. He gets reward for that (good) which he has earned, and he is punished for that (evil) which he has earned" (2:286)

Allah knows we are capable of obeying him and are able to deal with the passing away of our child. He knows what choices we will make. He is Al-Aleem (All-Knowing), but He does not compel us to act. We should realise that Allah is watching us and will bring us to account for our choices.

A believer who understands the concept of Qadr is very conscious of observing Allah's orders and fearing Him. A Muslim endeavours to comply with the commands of Allah and to abstain from the prohibitions, because of their fear of the punishment of Allah, their desire to be in Jannah, and their yearning in attaining that which is greater than all of this, namely the pleasure of Allah (Ridwaan Al-lah).

Qadr and grief

Let's now apply this understanding of Qadr to how we cope with the passing away of our child. I often hear grieving non-Muslim parents say, "If only the doctors had done xy or z. Or if only I had done things differently, then my child would still be alive", but that's not true. The day an adult or child is meant to pass away is fixed, it is in Allah's control. We must be crystal clear about what is in our sphere of control; we should not live our lives under the shadow of regret, guilt and what-ifs. Some Muslims hold unislamic views, which they will express to parents. I strongly recommend you ignore their insensitive comments because there is no Islamic evidence to justify them. Your child's death is not your fault; you are not be punished by Allah for your past sins. You could not have changed the destiny of your child.

What is in your control?

Let's take a look at what actions are in the sphere of your control if your child is ill or your child has passed away. These are the areas that you should concentrate on and spend time researching what

Allah and His Messenger say about them, so you can follow the guidance that has been given to you.

- You should always seek out medical treatment for your ill child.
- Gain Islamic knowledge about how the Prophet (saw) and the sahabah dealt with the death of their children.
- Visit your child's grave and make dua.
- Read Quran regularly.

To summarise, life and death happen by Allah's will because He has created us and controls everything; He knows all things even before they happen. But, we have the free choice to make decisions. Allah is so Merciful; He has given us guidance and solace via the sacred text and prophetic tradition so we can cope with the trauma of losing our child.

"There is no Muslim who calls upon his Lord with

a dua in which there is no sin or severing of family ties,

but Allah will give him one of three things:

Either He will answer his prayer quickly,

or He will store (the reward for) it in the Hereafter,

or He will divert an equivalent evil away from him."

They said: "We will say more dua."

He said: "Allah's bounty is greater."

(Tirmidhi)

THE POWER OF DUA

The only way you will truly be able to cope and begin to heal from the loss of your child is by making sincere dua. Think of dua as your new best friend. Dua is the first step to making sense of your heart-breaking experience. You should get into the habit of making dua regularly. We all know the power and importance of prayers, but sometimes we forget. For those of us living in liberal, secular societies such as the US and the UK, it's evident that religion plays only a cameo role. It's pushed to the periphery of life and just makes a brief appearance during christenings, weddings, and Christmas.

Unconsciously this mindset is influencing our thinking when it comes to making dua. Over time, in liberal states, a societal shift occurred; the role of religion is accepted but as a benign instrument, not as a guide in all walks of life. We are feeling the cultural consequences of that shift, so we sometimes forget to make dua.

How are we taught to solve our problems? By focusing on the supremacy of our individual talents and limitless potential. We are told to believe in ourselves, rely on our brainpower, skills, and knowledge. "You can do anything you set your mind to!" To rely on God is backward, old-fashioned, and unscientific. Unwittingly, we absorb these unrealistic ideas from popular culture and social media. But these empty slogans ignore our need for divine guidance.

Allah created us with two undeniable attributes: human fitrah and a mind to comprehend His existence. We have an inbuilt disposition to search for and recognise the Creator. We are not independent, self-sufficient beings. We need our Creator's help. We are weak and needy. Without water or warmth from the sun, we would be dead in approximately three to four days. We cannot cause rain to fall or the sun to rise. In the Quran, Allah encourages us to pause and ponder on His creation:

Indeed, in the creation of the heavens and the earth and the alternation of the night and the day are signs for those of understanding. (3:190)

And Allah has sent down rain from the sky and given life thereby to the earth after its lifelessness. Indeed, in that is a sign for a people who listen. (16:65)

Like Prophet Ibrahim (as), we search for the perfect Creator of the sun, moon, and stars. Alhamdulillah, through the Quran and Sunnah, Allah has blessed us with a system to sanctify Him. An essential part of that system is dua. Remember, you will never find perfection in yourself, nor can you solve your problems on your own. Navigating the swinging pendulum of life's highs and lows is no easy task. You need to utilise the most effective tool at your disposal and the best weapon in your arsenal: dua.

Let's remind ourselves of why dua is so powerful. Your Lord has proclaimed:

"Call upon Me, I will respond to you. Surely those who are too proud to worship Me will enter Hell, fully humbled." (40:60).

The Prophet (saw) said: "Supplication is worship itself." (Tirmidhi)

In his book, Shan al-Dua, Khattabi writes: "The meaning of dua is the servant asking his Lord for His Help, and asking His continued support. Its essence is that a person shows his neediness to Allah and frees himself from any power or ability to change (any matter by himself). This characteristic is a sign of servitude, and in it is the feeling of human submissiveness."

Abu Hurairah narrated that the Prophet (saw) said, "There is nothing more noble in the sight of Allah than dua" (Tirmidhi and Imam Ibn Majah).

When you engage in dua, you display the utmost humbleness and accept that no one can assist you except Allah. Therefore dua is the essence of worship. Allah declares in the Quran:

Say (O Muhammad): "My Lord pays attention to you only because of your dua to Him. But now you have indeed denied (Him). So the torment will be yours for ever (inseparable permanent punishment)." (25:77)

In his tafsir of the above ayah, Qurtabi writes that Allah is telling us: I have not created you because I have need for you, I have only created you so that you may ask Me, so I will forgive you and give you what you ask."

The Prophet (saw) said: "Your Lord, may He be blessed and exalted, is characterised by modesty and generosity, and He is so kind to His slave that, if His slave raises his hands to Him, He does not let him take them back empty." (Abu Dawood)

Umar had an excellent understanding of dua and that Allah is Al-Mujeeb (the One who responds). He once commented:
"I am not concerned whether Allah will respond to my call when I call Him or not. I know for a fact that if I ask Allah for something, He will give me that which is best for me. I am not worried on His part. Rather my concern and worry is on my part. Whether I will

put the effort to make dua, whether I will take action and exhaust the means to get my dua accepted. Because I know if I make dua while being certain and I take action, then Allah will certainly respond and give me that which is best for me."

In addition to Allah being Al-Mujeeb, He is also known as, Al-'Aleem (The All-Knowing), As-Samee' (The All-Hearing), Al-BaSeer (The All-Seeing) Al-Qareeb (The Very Close & Near).

The following Hadith Qudsi illustrates the power and majesty of Allah:

O, my slaves! If the first of you and the last of you, and the humans of you and the jinn of you were all to stand together in the same exact time and asked Me for something. And I were to give everyone what he or she requested, then that would not decrease nor diminish whatever I own and whatever I possess! Except what is decreased in the ocean when a needle is dipped into it. (Muslim)

The etiquette of making dua

Here are some guidelines and recommendations we should follow when making dua. Ibn al-Qayyim writes:

Dua and the seeking of protection from Allah are like weapons, but the sharpness of a weapon is not sufficient for it to cause effect, for the person that handles it also plays a role. So whenever the weapon is a perfect one, having no blemish in it, and the forearm is strong, and there are no preventing factors, then it will cause an effect on the enemy. But if any of these three factors are missing, then the effect will also be lessened. So, if the dua in and of itself is not correct, or the person making the dua has not combined between his heart and tongue in the dua, or if there is a preventing factor, then the desired effect will not occur. (Al-Da' wa al-Dawa')

Only Allah can answer your dua

You must fully believe that only Allah is capable of hearing your prayer, and only Allah has the power to grant you peace of mind and heal your broken heart. The Quran mentions this fact in (27:6) : "Who (else is there) that responds to the call of the one in distress when he calls out, and He removes evil (from him), and makes you inheritors of the earth? Is there any other God besides Allah? Little is it that you remember!"

Be mindful

When asking for the sorrow to not overwhelm you, pray to Allah with a sincere heart. Abu Hurairah narrated that the Prophet (saw) said, "Make dua to Allah in a state that you are certain that your dua will be responded to, and know that Allah does not respond to a dua that originates from a negligent, inattentive heart".(Tirmidhi)

Be in a state of wudu

One of the etiquettes of dua is that a person be in a state of wudu (ritual purity) while making dua. This is illustrated in the hadith of Abu Musa al-Ashari, in which he stated that the Prophet (saw) after the Battle of Hunayn, called for water, performed wudu, then raised his hands and said: "O Allah! Forgive Ubayd ibn Amir!"

Raise your hands

Amongst the etiquette of dua that is known by all Muslims, young or old, is that of raising one's hands while making dua. Abu Musa al-Ashaari, who narrated: "The Prophet (saw) made a dua, and I saw him raise his hands until I could see the whiteness of his armpits". And Ibn' Umar narrated: "The Prophet (saw) raised his hands and said: "O, Allah! I ask your protection for what Khalid has done!"

Face the Qiblah

Abdullah ibn Zayd narrated: "The Prophet (saw) left (Madinah) to this prayer place seeking rain. So he made a dua and asked for rain, then he faced the qiblah and turned his cloak inside-out". Imam al-Bukhari put this hadith in a chapter entitled, "Making dua facing the Qiblah," showing that it forms the etiquette of dua.

It has also been narrated that when the Quraysh tormented the Prophet (saw), he '...faced the Ka'bah and made a dua against them. So we are encouraged to turn towards the qiblah when we wish to make dua.

Send blessings upon the Prophet (saw)

The Prophet's (saw) said: "Every dua is covered until (the person) prays upon the Prophet (saw)". The dua is covered means that it is not raised up to Allah until the person making the dua accompanies it with the prayer upon the Prophet (saw). However, it seems that this is not an essential condition since the Prophet (saw) himself did not practice this all the time.

Pray with humility and fear

We must show humility to our Creator and humble ourselves before Him while making dua.

"Call upon your Lord with humility and in secret. Verily, He does not like the aggressors." (7:55)

Recite the names of Allah

"And to Allah belong the best names, so invoke Him by them. "(Quran 7:180)

When we contemplate the meaning of Allah's names, our love for Allah increases. The best way to appreciate the meaning of these names is to use the appropriate one when making dua. When you feel worried or hopeless, use Allah's name as-Salam (The Perfection and Giver of Peace). When you need Allah's guidance, invoke Allah's name al-Haadi (The Guide). If you are confused about how to explain death to young relatives in your family recite Allah's name al-Wakeel (The Trustee, The Disposer of Affairs) to help you make the correct decision. If you can no longer work and are worried about bills you have to pay, use Allah's name al-Razzaq (the One who Provides) and al-Ghani (the One who Gives and does not require anything). Whatever you are asking for, there is a divine name that you can use in your dua.

The best times to make dua

There are many specific times to make dua that have a higher chance of being accepted by Allah, as mentioned by the Prophet (saw). You should increase your dua during these times and start incorporating them into your daily routine immediately.

At the end of an obligatory salat

Begin a habit of making dua after your obligatory prayers. Narrated Abu Umamah: that Allah's Messenger (saw) was asked, O Messenger of Allah, which supplication is heard by Allah, he said at the end of the night and at the end of the obligatory Salat (Tirmidhi).

While prostrating

When you place your forehead on the ground in sujood, you are the closest to Allah. Abu Hurairah narrated that Allah's Messenger (saw) said: 'The nearest a slave can be to his Lord is when he is prostrating, so invoke (supplicate) Allah much in it. (Muslim)

The dua of a Muslim for his absent sister or brother

The Prophet (saw) said: 'There is no believing servant who supplicates for his brother in his absence where the angels do not say, 'the same be for you" (Muslim). If know of other parents who have also lost a child, make dua for them.

While visiting the sick

Umm Salamah narrated that the Prophet (saw) said: 'When you visit the sick, you should utter good words because the angels say 'Ameen' to whatever you say (Muslim)

Ali reported that the Prophet (saw) said: "When a Muslim visits his sick Muslim brother in the morning, seventy thousand angels make dua for his forgiveness till the evening. And when he visits him in the evening, seventy thousand angels make dua for his forgiveness till the morning, and he will be granted a garden for it in Jannah." (Tirmidhi).

The last third of the night

Abu Hurairah narrated that Allah's Messenger (saw) said: 'In the last third of every night our Rabb descends to the lowermost heaven and says; "Who is calling Me, so that I may answer him? Who is asking Me so that I may grant him? Who is seeking forgiveness from Me so that I may forgive him?."' (Sahih al-Bukhari, Hadith Qudsi).

Amr ibn Absah narrated that the Prophet (saw) said: 'The closest any worshipper can be to His Lord is during the last part of the night, so if you can be amongst those who remember Allah at that time, then do so'. (Tirmidhi).

The Prophet (saw) said: 'There is at night an hour, no Muslim happens to be asking Allah any matter of this world or the Hereafter, except that he will be given it, and this (occurs) every night.' (Muslim)

Between the adhan and iqamah

Anas narrated that Allah's Messenger (saw) said: 'A supplication made between the adhan and iqamah is not rejected.' (Ahmad)

When it is raining

Narrated Sahel Ibn Sa'ad: that the Messenger of Allah (saw) said: 'Two will not be rejected, Supplication when the Adhan (call of prayer) is being called, and at the time of the rain'. (Abu Dawud)

An hour on Friday

Narrated Abu Hurairah: Allah's Messenger (saw) said: 'There is an hour on Friday, and if a Muslim gets it while offering salat and asks something from Allah, then Allah will definitely meet his demand.' And he pointed out the shortness of that particular time with his hands. (Sahih, al-Bukhari). Some have said that this hour is from the time the Imam enters the masjid on Friday's prayer until the prayer is over (i.e. between the two khutbahs). Others have said that it is the last hour of the day, i.e., after the Asr prayer until the Maghrib prayer.

While drinking Zam zam water

Jaber narrated that Allah's Messenger (saw) said: 'Zam zam water is for what it is drunk for.' (Ahmad). This means that when you drink Zam zam water, you may ask Allah for anything you like to gain or benefit from this water.

Dua during the month of Ramadan

Ramadan is a sacred month in which making plentiful dua is highly encouraged. This can be inferred from the Prophet (saw) saying: "When Ramadan comes, the doors of paradise are opened, and the doors of hell are closed, and the shaitans are locked up." (Sahih al-Bukhari). It is clear that your dua during Ramadan has a greater chance of being accepted.

Dua of the one fasting until he breaks his fast

The Prophet (saw) said: Three supplications will not be rejected (by Allah), the supplication of the parent for his child, the supplication of the one who is fasting, and the supplication of the traveller. (Bayhaqi)

The Night Of 'Qadr' (Decree)

This night is the most incredible night of the year. This is the night about which the almighty Allah said, "The night of Al-Qadar (Decree) is better than a thousand months." (97: 3)

The night of decree is one of the odd nights of the last ten nights of the blessed month of Ramadan. The angels descend down to the earth, and the earth is overwhelmed with peace and serenity until the break of dawn, and when the doors of paradise are opened, the worshipper is encouraged to turn to Allah to ask for his needs for this world and the hereafter. Inshallah, may Allah answer all your duas and give you good in this life and the next. As I said at the start, dua should be your best friend, so use it to strive to gain peace of mind and relief from your sadness.

Suhaib reported: The Messenger of Allah (saw) said, "Strange is the affair of the mu'min (the believer), verily all his affairs are good for him. If something pleasing befalls him, he thanks (Allah), and it becomes better for him. And if something harmful befalls him, he is patient (sabir), and it becomes better for him. And this is only for the mu'min."

(Sahih Muslim)

PARTING MESSAGE

My dear brother/sister, I know that you are facing a great test; we have faced trials in the past, and we will face more in the future; the thing that will get us through our troubles is turning to Allah that's the only thing that will help us. When we ask Allah for help, He gives it; when we unburden our heart to Him, He listens. May every hardship you go through become a means of attaining closeness to Allah, may every loss you have suffered be a means of gaining His pleasure, may you be reunited with your loved ones in the akhirah in Jannat ul Firdous. Inshallah, please share this book with other parents who you think will gain solace from it. Inshallah, we will remember each other in our duas, asking Allah to make us patient and grateful. May Allah bless you with the best in deen, dunya, and akhirah.

Ameen

Farhat Amin

ABOUT THE AUTHOR

Farhat Amin is an author and host of the popular podcast Smart Muslima. She shares Islamic life advice via her website www.smartmuslima.com, to help women achieve confidence in their faith. The inspiration for both her website and podcast is Surah Asr:

"By Time. The human being is in loss. Except those who believe, and do good works, and encourage truth, and recommend patience."

She felt there was a need for a platform that represents Muslim women without falling into the temptation of watering down Islam for the sake of mass appeal. As Islam encourages hikmah (wisdom) when informing others of Islam, not compromise. You can follow her on instagram: farhatamin_uk. Inshallah if you have any queries about the book please email: hello@farhatamin.com.

Printed in Great Britain
by Amazon

31877977R00057